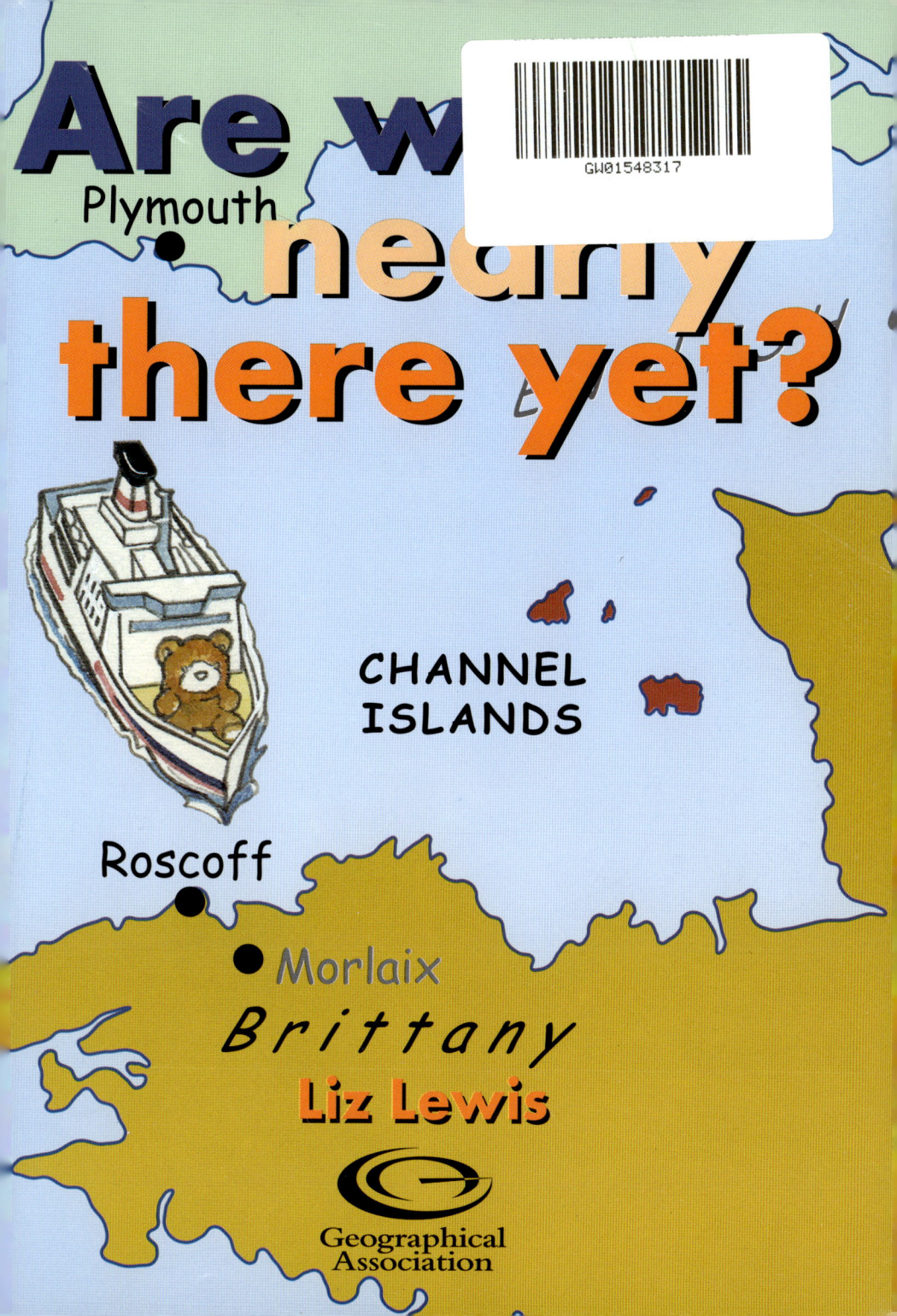

Barnaby is going to Brittany in France. He is going with Mum, Nan and Grandpa.

The ferry begins to move slowly out of the harbour.

'It will take about six hours,' says Mum.
'Sit down and have a rest, Barnaby.'

Barnaby looks out over the sea.
Now the town looks very small.

'Not yet,' says Nan, 'But it's time for lunch. Come and have something to eat, Barnaby.'

Barnaby is too excited to sit still and he gets up to look at the sea.

Mum takes Barnaby to the other side of the ferry to see if they can see France, but all he can see is the sea and another ferry.

Barnaby feeds some bread to the seagulls.

'Come and see, Barnaby!' says Mum,
'I can see France!'
'Hurray!' shouts Barnaby,
'We are nearly there!'